W9-AUD-539

HAMMOND CENTRAL
LIBRARY MEDIA CENTER
5925 Calumet Ave.
Hammond, Indiana 46320

976
OUE

Ouellette,
Jeannine.
Hurricane Katrina

BAR: 11P04127

PERMA-BOUND

DATE DUE			

Essential Events

HURRICANE
KATRINA

Essential Events

HURRICANE
KATRINA

BY JEANNINE OUELLETTE

Content Consultant
Dennis Feltgen, Meteorologist
NOAA—National Weather Service

ABDO
Publishing Company

CREDITS

Published by ABDO Publishing Company, 8000 West 78th Street, Edina, Minnesota 55439. Copyright © 2008 by Abdo Consulting Group, Inc. International copyrights reserved in all countries. No part of this book may be reproduced in any form without written permission from the publisher. The Essential Library™ is a trademark and logo of ABDO Publishing Company.

Printed in the United States.

Editor: Jill Sherman
Cover Design: Becky Daum
Interior Design: Lindaanne Donohoe

Library of Congress Cataloging-in-Publication Data
Ouellette, Jeannine.
  Hurricane Katrina / Jeannine Ouellette.
    p. cm. — (Essential events)
  Includes bibliographical references and index.
  ISBN-13: 978-1-59928-852-9
1. Hurricane Katrina, 2005. 2. Hurricane Katrina, 2005—Social aspects.
3. Hurricane Katrina, 2005—Economic aspects. 4. Hurricane Katrina, 2005—
Health aspects. 5. Emergency management—Louisiana—New Orleans. I. Title.
  QC945.O92 2008
  976'.044—dc22

                                                          2007012005

TABLE OF CONTENTS

Chapter 1

Max Mayfield of the National Hurricane Center monitors Hurricane Katrina.

THE APPROACHING STORM

On the morning of Saturday, August 27, 2005, the National Hurricane Center in Miami, Florida, issued the following statement:

...CATEGORY THREE KATRINA MOVING WESTWARD IN THE SOUTHEASTERN GULF

OF MEXICO ... EXPECTED TO TURN WEST NORTHWESTWARD AND STRENGTHEN ... AT 10 AM CDT ... 1500Z ... A HURRICANE WATCH IS IN EFFECT FOR THE SOUTHEASTERN COAST OF LOUISIANA EAST OF MORGAN CITY TO THE MOUTH OF THE PEARL RIVER ... INCLUDING METROPOLITAN NEW ORLEANS AND LAKE PONCHARTRAIN. A HURRICANE WATCH MEANS THAT HURRICANE CONDITIONS ARE POSSIBLE WITHIN THE WATCH AREA ... GENERALLY WITHIN 36 HOURS. A HURRICANE WATCH WILL LIKELY BE REQUIRED FOR OTHER PORTIONS OF THE NORTHERN GULF COAST LATER TODAY OR TONIGHT. INTERESTS IN THIS AREA SHOULD MONITOR THE PROGRESS OF KATRINA.[1]

Saffir–Simpson Scale

Scientists rate hurricanes for their strength on the Saffir-Simpson Scale. The scale is divided into five categories based on maximum sustained wind speeds. The higher the wind speed, the more powerful the hurricane. The National Hurricane Center designates a Category 3, 4, or 5 storm as a "major" hurricane, able to cause significant damage.

Saffir-Simpson Scale	
Category	Maximum Sustained Wind Speed
1	74-95 mph
2	96-110 mph
3	111-130 mph
4	131-155 mph
5	156 mph or greater

A hurricane—Katrina—was headed into the Gulf of Mexico. Over the previous two days, it had grown to a

Mayan Origins

The word "hurricane" dates back to the ancient Mayan name *Huracan*, one of the creator gods. When he blew his breath, he pushed back the water and created dry land. Throughout the Caribbean, the word came to mean "big wind."

Category 3 storm, a major hurricane. On a scale of one to five, as measured by scientists, a Category 3 hurricane packs winds of at least 111 miles per hour (178 km/h). Such powerful winds could rip trees out of the ground and tear roofs off houses. They could shatter glass, flip boats, and snap wooden power poles as if they were toothpicks.

Officially, scientists call a storm like a hurricane a Tropical Cyclone. The term "hurricane" is used for cyclones over the Atlantic Ocean and eastern Pacific Ocean. In the western Pacific, they are called "typhoons." In the Indian Ocean, they are "cyclones."

Along with its winds, Katrina threatened to deliver heavy rains. When it hit land, the rains could cause major flooding. The hurricane could also generate tornadoes, causing major damage as the storm moved inland. Worst of all, Katrina would bring with it a storm surge. A storm surge is a massive swell of ocean water—as high as 20 feet (6 m), sometimes even more. The surge is pushed toward the shore by whipping hurricane winds and the low air pressure in the

Inside the eye of Hurricane Katrina

hurricane eye. Wherever it struck, the surge would smash into the coastline with intense force.

TRACKING THE STORM

Katrina was a powerful storm and threatening to grow even worse. For more than two weeks, meteorologists and scientists at the National Hurricane Center watched a wave of tropical storms move westward off the coast of Africa. On the evening of August 23, the system had churned into the western Atlantic, just southeast of the Bahamian Islands. There, it pulled together, and satellite pictures recorded the first sign of massive rotation. Tropical Depression 12 had taken shape.

The National Hurricane Center

The National Hurricane Center (NHC) is in charge of tracking tropical storms and hurricanes and warning citizens of danger. The NHC is part of the National Oceanic and Atmospheric Administration (NOAA) and the National Weather Service (NWS). NOAA scientists study weather patterns and climate change and work on ways to better predict weather systems in the future.

Climatologists and meteorologists at the NHC predict, measure, and track hurricanes using a variety of tools. They use records of past weather conditions and patterns to help predict what will happen in future situations. They use radar and photographs taken by satellites to see hurricanes and track their paths. Hurricanes are also studied up close. Scientists fly aircraft near and over the cyclone and take measurements with highly sensitive instruments. This aircraft will drop measurement devices that send radio signals back to scientists directly into the storm.

All these efforts and instruments make for earlier and more accurate hurricane warnings. The more that is known about a hurricane, the better scientists at the NHC can predict the intensity and course of the hurricane.

By the next morning, a weather aircraft flying over the storm recorded growing winds. Clear spiral cloud bands had formed overnight. An inner core had also formed, and winds picked up speed quickly. The storm was over the Bahamas, following a slow path north and west, possibly toward central or northern Florida. Late that morning, Tropical Depression 12 was upgraded to Tropical Storm Katrina.

Tropical Storm Katrina was the eleventh storm in an already busy Atlantic hurricane season. Beginning on June 1, the Atlantic hurricane season continues until November 30. During this time ocean waters in the western Atlantic are warm enough to fuel tropical storms. By the time Tropical Storm Katrina came on the scene, four hurricanes had already occurred. Hurricanes Cindy, Dennis, and Emily had each taken its turn roaring through the Caribbean and the Gulf of Mexico. Hurricane Irene never made landfall. Meteorologists had predicted an active season. Ocean water temperatures were higher than average, and conditions were right for major storms to develop and move over the Atlantic. The Atlantic was also in the middle of a cycle of increased hurricane activity. Every 20 to 30 years, the region goes through weather pattern changes. Since 1995, tropical storm and hurricane activity had been higher than average. Even with this information, the intensity of the coming 2005 season was surprising.

Where Hurricanes Start

A hurricane is a massive storm formed over the ocean when unique weather and water conditions come together. The most important condition for a hurricane to form is warm ocean water, found in the tropics. The tropics are the region between the Tropic of Cancer (23.5° N latitude) and the Tropic of Capricorn (23.5° S latitude). All hurricanes form in this area.

Hurricane Winds

Hurricanes are known for their powerful, fast winds, sometimes reaching over 150 miles per hour (245 km/h). But the actual storm moves very slowly over the water. Like a bulldozer, a hurricane may move at less than ten miles per hour (16 km/h). That means a storm 500 miles (805 km) wide may take many hours to pass overhead, causing enormous damage.

By the morning of August 25, things were changing rapidly. Tropical Storm Katrina took a sudden turn westward. It headed straight for the southern tip of Florida, threatening to sweep over Miami. With its leading edge already over Florida, the storm gained a sudden burst of energy. Heavy winds whipped up, over 70 miles per hour (113 km/h). By that afternoon, just as the storm bore down on the tip of Florida, the National Hurricane Center upgraded Katrina to a Category 1 hurricane.

A little over six hours later, Hurricane Katrina had left Florida behind. The pounding was brief, but by the time it was over, 14 people had been killed in the storm. Unfortunately, as Katrina made it back out to sea, the worst was yet to come.

Tropical Storm Katrina gains power over the Atlantic Ocean.

New Orleans, Louisiana

A DELICATE BALANCE

he Crescent City, The Big Easy, the birthplace of jazz—New Orleans is known by many names. The city stands at the mouth of the great Mississippi River where the water fans out into a wide delta and flows into the Gulf of Mexico. Here, goods from throughout the United States meet ships headed across the globe. New Orleans is one of the largest ports in the world.

A Unique City

For 300 years, people have made their way to New Orleans. They blended their values, religions, and ideals together to make something new and special. The Spanish came first, followed by the French, then the English, immigrants from the Caribbean islands, and slaves from Africa. Out of this rich tapestry came unique customs, exotic foods, and diverse music and literature. New Orleans grew into a cultural capital known the world over, a place with an untamed, anything-can-happen side. It is a one-of-a-kind city. The great jazz trumpeter, Wynton Marsalis, calls New Orleans "a true American melting pot: the soul of America."[1]

But New Orleans is also a city in peril. New Orleans sits below sea level. Sea level is the point where the ocean waters meet land. From there, the land rises up, forming plains, hills, and mountains. But in some places, the land can actually dip back down. New Orleans is like that. It sits in a sort of hollow. And it is almost completely surrounded by water. On the north edge of the city is Lake Pontchartrain. Where the Gulf of Mexico meets Lake Borgne, two narrow straights link Pontchartrain to the sea. Wrapping around the south edge of the city is the Mississippi River. It winds its way from the west, making a wide curve around the central city, forming a "crescent," then bends east and south.

New Orleans is surrounded by high banks called "natural levees," which result from silt left behind after centuries of repeated flooding. A levee is a wall that holds water from spilling over into a lower lying area (from the French word *lever*, "to raise"). Some levees are natural, like the ones along rivers and lakes, and others are human made, often built from concrete many feet thick.

Behind the natural levees, where New Orleans sits between the Mississippi River and Lake Pontchartrain, the land is much lower. On average, New Orleans sits about six feet (2 m) below sea level. In most parts of the city, residents cannot actually see the water of the river or the lake. They would have to climb the high banks to do so.

That makes New Orleans like a giant bowl, surrounded by high walls. This bowl, home to nearly half a million people before Katrina, is below sea level. And the sea is only 50 miles away (80 km).

CAN YOU DEFEND AGAINST A HURRICANE?

With New Orleans situated below so much water, flooding has always been a danger. The Mississippi River and Lake Pontchartrain frequently overflow their banks. Even a heavy rain can swamp city streets. But the worst threat of all is the potential storm surge caused by a major hurricane. The bigger the storm, the higher the wall of water, possibly as high as 30 feet (9 m). A swell of water pushed ahead by a hurricane could blast into Lake Pontchartrain or up the Mississippi and spill into the city, filling it up like a bathtub.

Engineers and scientists have wrestled with New Orleans' flood threat for more than 200 years. Back in the 1800s, the city built large earthen embankments, like the natural levees, in many areas around the city. Pumps were installed to draw up floodwaters and push them back into lakes and rivers. Throughout the 1900s, the city built high concrete floodwalls along Lake Pontchartrain, the Mississippi River, and other waterways. Engineers also dug channels and built reservoirs to contain water flow and improve drainage.

Flood Control

By 2000, New Orleans was surrounded by a flood control system that included 520 miles (832 km) of levees, 270 floodgates, 92 pumping stations, and thousands of miles of drainage canals.

After each major storm, they built walls higher, made them stronger, and constructed more.

DIRE PREDICTIONS

Despite the continuous efforts of scientists and

A History of Troubles

For two centuries, New Orleans has built its walls higher and stronger. But time and again, nature has proven a powerful force. Repeatedly, hurricanes have pummeled the region, with many lives lost to floods and storm surges. Some of the more notable hurricanes are listed below:

❖ August 14, 1901—A hurricane strikes at Buras and Port Eads. Every building in Port Eads is destroyed except the lighthouse.

❖ September 29, 1915—A hurricane strikes near New Orleans, where winds reach 130 miles per hour (159 km/h). Storm surges of more than 12 feet (3.5 m) strike north of Grand Isle. At least 275 people are killed.

❖ June 27, 1957—Hurricane Audrey causes waves of 40–50 feet (12–18 m) with sustained winds of 145 miles per hour (209 km/h). The storm kills at least 526 people.

❖ August 18, 1969—Hurricane Camille is one of the most intense storms on record at the time. It causes a 16-foot (4.5 m) storm surge along much of southeast Louisiana.

❖ September 10–13, 1998—Tropical Storm Frances makes landfall north of Corpus Christi, Texas, then tracks north to Dallas. Heavy rain causes flooding in New Orleans.

engineers to protect New Orleans with an improved levee system, the chance of a major hurricane smashing the city never went away. Many building projects that began in the 1970s to make New Orleans safe from a Category 3 storm were still unfinished in 2005.

Engineers said New Orleans and the rest of the country were ignoring a disaster waiting to happen. In 2001, *Scientific American* magazine published an article entitled "The Drowning of New Orleans." The story laid out the case that a major hurricane making a direct strike could easily swamp the city. Even with all the engineering of the past 40 years, a storm surge could jump the levee system and "drown New Orleans under twenty feet of water," said Joe Suheday, a retired engineer from Louisiana State University, two years before Katrina. "I don't think people realize how precarious we are."[2]

Catastrophes

In 2001, the Federal Emergency Management Agency (FEMA), issued a list of the three worst catastrophes that could strike the United States: a major earthquake in San Francisco, a terrorist attack in New York City, and a hurricane swamping New Orleans.

To make matters worse, scientists pointed to new developments that have made New Orleans even more vulnerable than before. Global warming was a growing concern because of rising sea levels, and the warmer water temperatures could feasibly provide more fuel for hurricanes, making them stronger and larger.

Experts also noted that the bowl that makes up New Orleans was sinking. While the city is already below sea level, it continues to sink every year (known as "subsidence") and will drop another three feet (1 m) by the next century. In addition, the city's canals seep water back into the ground, and pumps must constantly bring water up from underground and move it out. At this rate, New Orleans in the future will be even easier to fill and harder to dry out.

But the most severe problem facing the region is actually the result of the efforts to protect it. The Mississippi River carried silt that, when deposited into the Gulf of Mexico, created small islands and thousands of square miles of sandy beaches and marshes. It built a natural barrier between New Orleans and the sea.

With the flood control system around New Orleans, the Mississippi has been increasingly cut off from the coastline. The barrier islands have diminished and ocean tides have eaten away beaches and killed freshwater grasses that hold the shore together. In the past 70 years, Louisiana has lost 1,900 square miles (4,900 sq km) of protective shore. Experts estimate that by 2090, the Mississippi delta will be gone, leaving New Orleans sitting at the very edge of the ocean.

All these factors combined have made New Orleans more vulnerable than ever before. As a result, many leading geologists were of the belief that it was only a matter of time before disaster struck.

A Direct Hit

For years experts warned of catastrophe. If a major hurricane of enough size and intensity made a direct hit on New Orleans, a storm surge could breach the levees. It might even break through floodwalls. If either happened, New Orleans would be under several feet of water. The city could be virtually destroyed, and thousands of people might die.

In 1965, Hurricane Betsy bashed New Orleans with winds up to 30 miles per hour (208 km/h). Its eye passed just a few miles west of the city. The storm surge breached floodwalls along the major Mississippi River canal leading to the Gulf. Then, floodwalls broke in several spots, and within hours, many neighborhoods were under ten feet (3 m) of water. Hurricane Betsy killed 58 people in Louisiana and caused over $1 billion in damage.

As a result of Betsy, the federal government spent millions of dollars to improve and heighten levee walls

Subsidence

As the land subsides within New Orleans, it weakens floodwalls and the concrete channel system from below. If a wall were to break during a hurricane, millions of gallons of water would instantly pour into the city. J. David Rogers, chairman of geological engineering at the University of Missouri-Rolla, predicted before Katrina, "If one (levee) opens up, they open so quickly there's nothing you can do from an engineering response. It'll be over within 10 minutes."[3]

New Orleans Population

Before Katrina the population of New Orleans was more than 450,000 with approximately 1.3 million people living in the metropolitan area.

around New Orleans. The U.S. Army Corps of Engineers, the federal government's lead engineering body, led the way to improving New Orleans' flood control system. They worked continuously to build more levees, trying to control nature as best they could. Using new measuring tools and hurricane models to predict possible storm surges, they planned to extend the height of many floodwalls.

Even so, many who remembered Hurricane Betsy were ready to leave on August 27. The Army Corps of Engineers declared the city able to withstand a Category 3 hurricane the size of Betsy. But a declaration is not proof. No one could say if all that work and money was really enough. And what about a Category 4 or 5 hurricane? What then? Meanwhile, on August 27, 2005, as the day progressed, Hurricane Katrina was growing.

After Hurricane Betsy hit New Orleans in 1965, the federal government focused on improving the city's floodwalls.

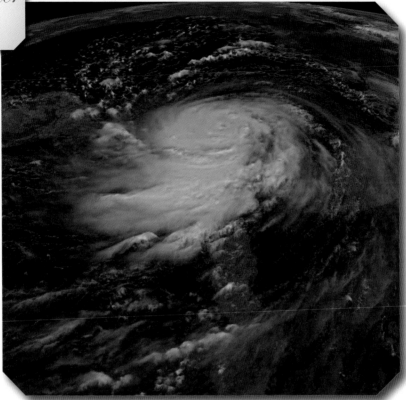

Chapter 3

Hurricane Katrina gained power over the Gulf of Mexico.

FLIGHT FROM DANGER

After hitting southern Florida, Katrina was back out to sea by August 26. The storm was ready to pick up more power. The Gulf of Mexico's waters, even warmer than the western Atlantic, provided perfect fuel for a hurricane still gathering strength.

Out over open water, Katrina rapidly expanded. The inner eye became more distinct. Readings showed signs of increased activity near the core. The storm's spiral arms stretched out further from the eye. Storm intensity picked up, with winds bursting to more than III miles per hour (178 km/h). On August 27, over a span of less than 18 hours, Katrina jumped from a Category I to a Category 3 hurricane.

Now, Katrina was twice as big as it had been when it hit Florida. Tropical storm winds extended more than 280 miles (448 km/h) across the hurricane. A Category 3 hurricane packs an incredible punch, and the National Hurricane Center alerted federal, state, and emergency officials that Katrina could cause severe damage wherever it made landfall. But the question was, where would it strike? Hurricanes are notorious for changing direction. Its course pointed toward Texas or Mexico. But meteorologists knew a weather system moving in from the north could block Katrina's path and push it northward. If it did, the hurricane would head straight for New Orleans.

Hurricanes in the Gulf

Hurricanes often strengthen when they move from the Atlantic Ocean into the Gulf of Mexico. That is because the water is often warmer in the Gulf. Warm water temperatures send water vapor more quickly up into the hurricane's turbulent core.

That is exactly what it did. By the night of August 26, Katrina turned toward the northwest. The National Hurricane Center issued a frightening warning:

> *... DANGEROUS HURRICANE KATRINA*
> *THREATENS THE NORTH CENTRAL GULF*
> *COAST ... A HURRICANE WARNING ISSUED ...*
>
> *PREPARATIONS TO PROTECT LIFE AND*
> *PROPERTY SHOULD BE RUSHED TO*
> *COMPLETION.[1]*

With Katrina suddenly growing to a Category 3 storm and taking aim on New Orleans, the governor of Louisiana, Kathleen Blanco, declared a "state of emergency" on August 26. She called on National Guard troops to set up evacuation routes and assist residents to leave coastal areas. By the morning of August 27, Haley Barbour, the governor of Mississippi, had also declared a state of emergency for his state. At the request of Governor Blanco, President George W. Bush authorized the Federal Emergency Management Agency (FEMA), "to coordinate all disaster relief efforts which have the purpose of alleviating the hardship and suffering caused by the emergency on the local population, and to provide appropriate assistance for required emergency measures."[2] FEMA, which operates under The Department of Homeland Security (DHS), handles disaster situations.

Out in the Gulf, oil rigs were shut down and ships were diverted to other ports. The region is responsible for 25 percent of the nation's oil and gas production. Scientists predicted Hurricane Katrina could severely damage production and disrupt the port system in and around New Orleans.

Katrina was clearly closing in on New Orleans, and the warm waters of the Gulf provided Katrina with plenty of fresh fuel. By midnight, Katrina went through another powerful intensification. Satellite images recorded the eye forming into a tight, well-defined ring, a sign of increased strength. Winds picked up even more, and the storm widened.

Naming Storms

Scientists in the U.S. began naming tropical cyclones during World War II to keep easier track of multiple storms moving about the Atlantic and Pacific Oceans at the same time. Naming made for quick reference. The first named storm was George, but its title was unofficial. Hurricane Bess was named in 1949 after First Lady Bess Truman, President Harry Truman's wife. The National Weather Service began officially using names in 1953. Until 1979, the service only designated storms with women's names. After 1979, they applied both men's and women's names.

EVACUATE!

The morning of August 28, Katrina burst into a Category 5 hurricane. Its maximum sustained winds roared to 175 miles per hour (280 km/h) as the monster slowly marched toward New Orleans.

During the three days prior to landfall, the National Hurricane Center had warned that Katrina could take aim directly on New Orleans. The National Hurricane Center's director, Max Mayfield, personally called the governors of Louisiana and Mississippi as well as New Orleans' mayor, Ray Nagin. At 9:30 a.m., the mayor announced the first-ever mandatory evacuation of New Orleans. He declared that all residents had to leave the city for their own safety. He said,

> I wish I had better news, but we're facing the storm most of us have feared. This is very serious. This is going to be an unprecedented event.[3]

Governor Blanco, standing with the mayor, added,

> We need to get as many people out as soon as possible.[4]

Just after 10:00 a.m. local time on the morning of August 28, the National Weather Service issued a terrifying warning. It called Katrina "a most powerful hurricane with unprecedented strength ... rivaling the intensity of hurricane Camille of 1969." It warned of extreme winds and devastating damage, "most of the area will be uninhabitable for weeks ... perhaps longer."[5]

But evacuation was going to be a problem. New Orleans has only a few major highways leading in or out of the city, and roadways had been packed since the day before. With precious hours ticking by, authorities reversed traffic on the inbound lanes of major roadways in an effort to double capacity and flow traffic in one direction—away from the city. This helped, but traffic was still slow moving. The mayor called on residents with cars to help those without transportation. He called on residents of New Orleans to work together more than they ever have before.

All along the Louisiana and Mississippi coasts, towns and

Emergency Workers

Hundreds of emergency shelters were set up inland in Louisiana and Mississippi. Emergency workers filled school gyms, government buildings, and hospitals with cots and blankets, preparing for the flood of people in need of a place to stay. In all, more than 75,000 people sought refuge in emergency shelters. Hotels in the northern parts of both states, as well as in Texas, were also booked solid with evacuees.

Medical centers and special shelters in the region prepared to take on chronically ill and disabled evacuees who were sent from New Orleans hospitals. Thousands of workers and volunteers filled sandbags along riverbanks. The storm was expected to dump five to ten inches (13 to 25 cm) of rain on the region, causing flash floods in several low-lying areas.

counties (or "parishes" as they are known in Louisiana) declared evacuations. People boarded up their homes and fled. First responders stayed behind to prepare for Katrina's onslaught and later to dig out from under the damage. In all, more than one million people evacuated the New Orleans metropolitan area, but thousands stayed behind.

SHELTER OF LAST RESORT

Many of the city's poorest residents were stranded with no way to get out. They had no vehicles of their own and could not find other means to travel. "I know they're saying 'Get out of town,' but I don't have any way to get out. If you don't have no money, you can't

---

Waiting for Shelter

About 10,000 people headed for the Superdome stadium before the storm. As people stood in line, waiting to get inside, the mood ran from festive to fearful.

Michael Skipper stood with a wagon loaded with clothes and a radio. "We just took the necessities. The good stuff—the television and the furniture—you just have to hope something's there when you get back. If it's not, you just start over."[6]

Another man, Joey Branson, walked in with a fresh-baked apple pie and a mystery novel. He said, smiling, "That's all I need. I'm set for the duration."[7]

But others were more fearful. "I just want a place I can be quiet and left alone," said Curtis Cockran. He sat waiting in his wheelchair after a recent hip surgery. "I don't know if I'll have a place to go back to, but there's no reason to worry about that now. For the time being I just want to be safe."[8]

go,"said Hattie Johns, age 74.[9] For Hattie, and others like her, the options were bad and getting worse by the minute. City officials decided to open the New Orleans Superdome and nine other smaller sites as "shelters of last resort."

Flooding

In recent years, more people have been killed by flooding than by all other storm effects combined, even surges.

The Superdome, one of the largest buildings in the country, is a massive indoor stadium, 20 stories high, with 77,000 seats. Architects believed it to be a strong structure, capable of withstanding hurricane force winds. It was on some of the highest ground in the city.

Mayor Nagin advised people going to the Superdome to bring clothing, water, and enough food to last three or four days. It was likely the building would be out of power for at least that long, and there was no telling when residents could return to their homes. Governor Blanco sent more than 500 National Guard troops to secure the building. They brought three truckloads of water and seven truckloads of Meals Ready to Eat, enough to feed 15,000 people for three days.

On August 28, throughout the day, city buses picked up people around the city and brought them to the Superdome. Thousands more walked across town in sweltering late-summer heat, carrying backpacks or pushing shopping carts full of their belongings. Adults, children, and the elderly lined the entrance. They stood in line for upwards of five hours to get inside the building, even as the rains came pelting down. By the end of the day, an estimated 26,000 people—all fearing for their lives—had made their way to the Superdome.

New Orleans was in a frenzy. Buildings and businesses shut down. Hospitals and nursing homes moved as many patients as possible out of the city to area hospitals further inland. Those who could not be transported out of town were moved to higher floors. Emergency workers went on full alert. Officials ordered a curfew for Sunday evening.

Still, there were those who refused to leave their homes, even in the face of terrifying predictions. Some believed they could brave out the storm. Many feared their homes would be looted after Katrina passed.

Others refused to believe the worst could actually happen and chose to remain in the city. By nightfall, heavy showers fell and winds increased. Hurricane Katrina showed no signs of losing power.

Even as the storm hit New Orleans, residents made their way to the Superdome.

Flooding in New Orleans began on August 29.

LANDFALL

On Monday, August 29, Katrina made a sudden turn east. Nudged again by the northern high pressure over the Midwest, the storm veered just slightly from a direct strike on New Orleans. But Katrina was raging as a Category 5 storm. Forecasters predicted Katrina would make landfall in less than 12 hours. Landfall is the point when the eye of the hurricane first makes contact with land. The storm was immense, with hurricane force winds extending 110 miles (177 km) to the east and 60 miles (96 km) to the west of the center. A slight shift to the east would make little, if any, difference.

Katrina pushed slowly toward Louisiana's southernmost coastline into Sunday night. The outer spiral of storm clouds and damaging winds slammed evacuated coastal delta towns. With the winds came high waves plowed ahead by the advancing storm surge.

At about 4:00 a.m., winds dropped slightly to around 150 miles per hour (241 km/h), making Katrina a Category 4 storm. The drop in wind speed hardly made a difference as enormous waves, which had built up over the previous two days, crashed onto the coastal plain. When the storm was less than 100 miles out to sea, waves were recorded as high as 55 feet (16 m). And the waves kept coming, one after another.

On the News

The nation watched as dramatic television images rolled in. Reporters with major networks stationed along the north Louisiana coast from New Orleans, Louisiana, to Biloxi, Mississippi, provided frightening footage. As Katrina struck land hundreds of miles to the south, heavy rains poured down on New Orleans and waves battered the shoreline.

Then, at 6:10 a.m. local time, Hurricane Katrina made landfall. It struck near Grand Isle, just west of the mouth of the Mississippi River—about 70 miles (112 km) southeast of New Orleans. Katrina blasted the area with sustained winds of about 130 miles per hour (209 km/h), falling between a low Category 4 or high Category 3 storm at exact landfall. But already, for four hours, hurricane winds and waves had pummeled inland areas as far as New Orleans and Biloxi, Mississippi.

A storm surge upwards of 28 feet (8.5 m) smashed into the coast. The swell of water, rising

Pinpoint Accuracy

Weather forecasters do not have an easy time predicting where a hurricane will make its final landfall. Many factors can cause a storm to change course at the last minute. The average margin of distance a hurricane usually moves from the time of prediction is 99 miles (159 km) with 48 hours before landfall. But scientists at the National Hurricane Center and the National Weather Service predicted Hurricane Katrina's landfall to within 15 miles (24 km) of its actual strike. More than three days before Katrina hit Louisiana, they predicted that New Orleans lay in the storm's path. The National Hurricane Center also predicted Katrina's strength at landfall to within 10 miles per hour (16 km/h).

Still, some people argue that the warnings did not come soon enough. They suggest more people could have evacuated New Orleans if they had more time. However, most of the people who remained behind did not have an easy means to leave the city. They lacked transportation of their own. Many also decided to ride out the storm, believing it would not be as bad as forecasted. Even with an earlier warning, many people may have had a very hard time finding a way to evacuate.

not like a wall but more like a giant mound, virtually swallowed Louisiana towns like Buras and Empire, leaving nearly every structure flattened or ripped from its foundation.

Having ravaged the southern coast, Hurricane Katrina continued directly northward. It kept to its slow, steady pace and still held onto its Category 3 strength over the Mississippi River peninsula. Though hurricanes often weaken over land, Katrina was so massive and wide that it barely lost any energy over the next few hours. In fact, Katrina caused storm surges for hundreds of miles to the east and west. Even as far away as the Florida panhandle, Katrina pushed a swell six to eight feet tall (2–2.4 m) over the coast.

The Eye

Katrina's eye was more than 30 miles (48 km) wide. Hurricane winds extended for nearly 75 miles (120 km) to the east and 60 miles (96 km) to the west as it inched toward New Orleans.

KATRINA PRESSES NORTH

Around 8:00 a.m., Katrina roared over St. Bernard Parish, just east of New Orleans. Floodwaters poured in every direction. The storm surge pushed a mass of water up the Mississippi River and across low-lying areas to the east. A 19-foot (5.7-m) swell struck St. Bernard Parish and the east side of New Orleans.

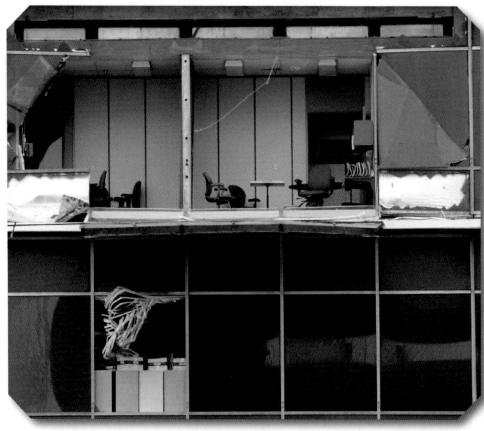

Windows are blown out on a building in downtown New Orleans as Hurricane Katrina batters Louisiana on Monday, August 29, 2005.

Katrina had weakened only slightly in its few hours over southeast Louisiana. Still charging ahead, it soon rolled out over the open gulf waters of Lake Borgne. There, Katrina held its strength, with Category 3-force winds and wind gusts measured at over 150 miles per hour (241 km/h).

It continued its slight eastward movement, away from New Orleans, but battered the city with continuing rains and winds that shattered windows in high-rise buildings. As early as 5:00 a.m., power started going out across the city. The Superdome lost power, too. Its emergency generators kicked in with lights but could not run the air conditioning.

Between 9:00 and 10:00 a.m., Katrina made its second landfall. It smashed the northern Louisiana and Mississippi coasts where the two states meet. Winds barreled at a Category 3 force. The storm surge rolled in at 28 feet (8.5 m).

Measurements

Exact measurements of storm surges and flooding were made difficult in some areas, as so much equipment was either destroyed or failed due to loss of electricity.

The surge pumped west into Lake Pontchartrain. It rushed over the low-lying bridges of Interstate 10 and Highway 90, which connect New Orleans to the northeast Louisiana coast. The water, pushing like a bulldozer, smashed whole sections of both bridges away.

Katrina forced heavy winds from the east and north, ramming the surge back across Pontchartrain and toward New Orleans. When it hit the south edge of Lake Pontchartrain, at the city's walls, the mass of water was still 15 feet (4.5 m) above normal.

Did New Orleans Dodge a Bullet?

With early signs that Katrina veered eastward, away from a direct hit over New Orleans, news reports pointed out the city would be spared the worst of the storm. The eye, where the strongest winds and heaviest rains centered, passed by New Orleans, about 20 miles (32 km) east of the city.

Reports that morning from inside New Orleans offered little information. Reporters had to go indoors for safety, and the heavy rains broke up broadcast

Surge

The surge spread the sea six miles (10 km) inland, and 12 miles (19 km) up rivers and bays. Along the coast, the 28-foot (8.5 m) monster surge stretched for 20 miles (32 km), from the Louisiana-Mississippi border east to Gulfport. Farther east and west, the mountain of water sloped lower and lower. It stretched for hundreds of miles.

signals. The rest of the country could only watch and wait. As Katrina moved north, some reporters announced the worst was over. Just after the storm passed, images from higher-ground areas, such as the Garden District, showed no sign of heavy flooding. Some television and radio news networks suggested that New Orleans had "dodged a bullet." They were wrong.

Floodwaters covered a portion of New Orleans after Katrina passed through the city.

Floodwaters pour through a levee near New Orleans.

Disaster

When Katrina pushed toward St. Bernard Parish, its storm surge plowed up the Mississippi River, sending a mass of water more than 20 feet (6 m) high toward New Orleans. By dawn, water overtopped the Mississippi River Gulf Outlet (MRGO) channel walls, only

15 feet (4.5 m) tall in most spots, spilling into both Saint Bernard Parish and east New Orleans. Mayor Nagin, speaking on a television morning news show, announced,

> *I've gotten reports this morning that there is already water coming over some of the levee systems. In the Lower Ninth Ward, we've had one of our pumping stations stop operating, so we will have significant flooding, it is just a matter of how much.[1]*

No one knew at the time just how bad the problem was. Within an hour of the reports of overtopping, the surge breached the MRGO channel. Breaching occurred in not one but several spots along a six-mile (9.6 km) corridor of the channel. The surge also broke through Mississippi levees farther south in Plaquemines Parish. The flood lifted houses off their foundations and tossed them aside.

Water Rising

Chris Robinson spoke with a reporter by cell phone. He stood in the attic of his home somewhere east of downtown. "The water's rising pretty fast. I got a hammer and an ax and a crowbar, but I'm holding off on breaking through the roof until the last minute. Tell someone to come get me please. I want to live."[2]

News Reports

Adaora Udoji, a CNN correspondent stationed near downtown New Orleans, described the storm's power, "…we were outside for just a few minutes. And it literally sounds like the streets are screaming. It's even beyond howling. And you can hear everything rocking down the street. You can hear garbage cans. Street signs have been ripped off. And it just seems to be getting worse, I mean, rapidly in the last ten or fifteen minutes."[3]

Farther ahead, another breach erupted where the MRGO Channel linked to the Intercoastal Waterway on the eastern edge of New Orleans. The Intercoastal Waterway is a narrower passage. It acted like a funnel with the surge jamming into the narrower opening. Water broke through both east and west, driving into St. Bernard Parish, eastern New Orleans, and the Upper and Lower Ninth Wards. This was even before Katrina's eye finished passing the city.

The surge was not finished. It rushed into the Intercoastal Waterway and ran headlong into the Industrial Canal, the main shipping channel between the Mississippi and Lake Pontchartrain. The Industrial Canal is like the top of a T with the Intercoastal Waterway as the stem. Katrina's 20-foot waters (6 m) slammed in, overtopping, then breaching, levee walls into central New Orleans. Only blocks ahead, two more breaches erupted along the Industrial Canal, just where it runs along the Lower Ninth Ward. The enormous breaks allowed even more water to flow into the already-flooded neighborhood. By 11:00 a.m., most of St. Bernard Parish looked like a lake.

The worst really had arrived. But it was far from over. Thousands who had remained behind were caught in the rising flood. Reports came of people struggling on foot through knee-deep water, intense rains, and driving wind in search of higher ground. Others stayed indoors—trapped. By midday, water reached rooflines throughout the Lower Ninth Ward.

While the surge flowed in from the east, Katrina pummeled New Orleans with sustained winds of over 125 miles per hour (200 km/h). It tore open rooftops and toppled 200-year-old trees. Electric power went down across the city. The winds blew out windows in office towers and hotels. One side of the Hyatt Regency Hotel's glass exterior was virtually ripped away by the wind. Its windows crashed to the street like giant raindrops.

At the Superdome, the building shook and rattled under constant winds. Power had gone out at dawn. Generators kept the lights on, but the machines could not handle the 9,000 tons of air conditioning equipment needed to keep the dome cool. Swampy, damp heat crept into the building. Even as the heaviest winds blew, people still arrived seeking shelter.

Around 9:30 a.m., with Katrina at its strongest, the winds peeled away large sections of the dome's roof. Two pieces, each approximately 5 by 15 feet (1.5 by 4.6 m) were torn off near the top of the dome. The thousands who had fled to the dome seeking safety now looked up in horror as rain poured into the building.

The National Guard quickly cleared the area under the exposed dome. Refugees from the storm huddled together amongst brightly colored orange, purple, and teal seats. Instead of feeling safe, many feared for their lives.

Information Breakdown

With power down and even first responders and reporters off the streets, information about Katrina was hard to come by once the storm struck. Even those television and radio stations able to operate on emergency power had little to tell on the morning of August 29. It was simply too dangerous to go out into the storm. Rescue workers first reported the levee breaches that morning.

As information slowly traveled from one official to another, conflicting reports emerged. Reporting by the major television networks picked up anything they could, but then found it hard to sort between facts and speculation. As the day wore on, the problem grew worse. Some reports claimed New Orleans had suffered only moderate damage.

The chaos of information that began on Monday only grew worse over the following days. Officials from dozens of departments made conflicting statements. Rumors ran rampant. News reports told frightening stories of murder and looting throughout the city. Some turned out to be true, but most were not.

The Storm Surge Widens

The storm surge rushed into wide-open Lake Borgne. With Hurricane Katrina's eye passing directly over the lake, a 25-foot (7.6 m) swell poured west and north. Within minutes, just as forecasters had feared, the surge plowed into Lake Pontchartrain. By the time the mass of water slammed into the levees along the south shore, the surge was still more than 15 feet (4.5 m) high.

At the Superdome

"It shook—the dome shook!" said Willanne Hughes. "I felt pretty safe, but my daughter didn't. I told her to start praying."[4]

Surprisingly, levees along the lake held, with only moderate overtopping. Instead, their strength served to funnel a tremendous force of water into the canals leading from Lake Pontchartrain to New Orleans. Just as with the Intercoastal Waterway, water jammed its way into the handful of narrow inlets stemming from the lake. Again, the surge overtopped levees at the canals, dumping water into New Orleans from the north.

In no time, the pressure was too much. At the 17th Street Canal on the city's far west side, water breached the levee within blocks of the lake. The flood created a wide opening along one side of the canal facing the inner city.

Some time later, the London Avenue Canal breached. The canal, leading from Pontchartrain into the central city, broke in two places. Unfortunately, the breaks occurred on each side, allowing water to pour both east and west.

The Flood

The east side of New Orleans was already flooded by the initial storm surge. Then, the breach at the Industrial Canal opened the central city to floodwaters. Now, with the new breaches, water poured in along the west side and into the heart of New Orleans.

But the breaches at the 17th Street and London Avenue canals opened a new and far worse problem for New Orleans. The flooding was not just from the storm surge. This was Lake Pontchartrain. Lake water swamped through the broken floodwalls. New Orleans was truly filling up like a bowl. ⌒

*Many parts of New Orleans remained flooded
long after Hurricane Katrina had passed.*

Chapter 6

Rescuers help those stranded on their rooftops reach dry land.

DESTRUCTION

The first surge swamped St. Bernard Parish and the east side of New Orleans as early as 8:00 a.m, August 30. Less than two hours after the levees had breached, ten feet (3 m) of water surrounded tens of thousands of homes.

When the surge off Lake Pontchartrain breached

levees at the 17th Street and London Avenue Canals,
the second wave of flooding moved in more slowly.
The breaks in the levees acted like a slow drain, allowing
the lake to pour in, but it had a very large bowl to fill.
By midday, many areas on the west side were knee-deep
in water. Later that afternoon, five feet (1.5 m) of water
stood around some buildings. The problem was that
Lake Pontchartrain was not going to stop pouring in
anytime soon. Into the night, as the storm cleared, the
water kept rising.

DAMAGE ALONG THE COAST

Katrina caused devastating damage
all along the northeast Louisiana
coast, across Mississippi and Alabama,
even causing flooding and destruction
on the Florida panhandle. Water
engulfed towns like Slidell on the
north rim of Lake Pontchartrain.

St. Bernard Parish

St. Bernard Council Chairman Joey DiFatta announced, "Water is inundating everywhere."[1]

Sixty miles (96 km) inland, Baton Rouge was whipped
with winds at 50 miles per hour (80 km/h).

Along the Mississippi coast, the gigantic surge
nearly crushed beautiful shoreline cities like Bay Saint
Louis, Long Beach, Gulfport, and Biloxi. This is
where Katrina was at its most destructive. Homes and

businesses were flattened by 125-mile-per-hour (201 km/h) sustained winds. The 28-foot surge (8.5 m) tossed buildings, cars, and boats miles inland, piling them atop each other like toys. Hurricane Katrina had

torn coastal bridges to pieces. After the storm passed, numerous fires broke out, adding to the destruction. Millions of viewers across the world watched as footage, taken just hours after Katrina struck, revealed the horrible devastation. As Katrina moved inland, it dropped to a Category 2 hurricane, then down to Category 1. But even then, the storm raged. It spawned 11 tornados

Mayor C. Ray Nagin

As mayor of New Orleans, Ray Nagin stood at the center of attention as Hurricane Katrina took aim on his city. His call for a mandatory evacuation was the first in the city's history. But he was immediately criticized for not having a plan to remove the estimated 100,000 poor and elderly without vehicles or other transportation.

Nagin turned the criticism on others in the days after the storm. He pointed blame at President Bush and the heads of Homeland Security and the Federal Emergency Management Agency for their response to the disaster.

Unfortunately, Nagin also whipped up fears and racial tensions as he predicted 10,000 dead in New Orleans. He said on the *Oprah Winfrey Show* that "hundreds of armed gang members" roamed the Superdome, killing and raping victims. He said the crowd there had fallen into an "almost animalistic state."[7] Neither claim was true. He also suggested the problems with delivering relief to his stricken city were caused by white racism toward a largely poor African-American population.

Months after the disaster, opinions remained divided over Nagin's leadership, but in May 2006, he was re-elected mayor of New Orleans.

in Mississippi, 11 more in Alabama, and 20 in Georgia. Four to eight inches (10 to 20 cm) of rain fell over much of Mississippi.

Back in New Orleans, the breach at the 17th Street Canal crumbled into a 200-foot (60 m) gap. Estimates came of 100,000 people still stranded in the city, tens of thousands with their homes under water. Power had gone out. The drinking water system was down. Dozens of pumping stations had failed. City Council President Oliver Thomas looked out over the Lower 9th Ward where he grew up and could not believe what he was seeing. No one had seen anything like it before. Meanwhile, the water kept rising.

RISING WATERS

On the east side of New Orleans, hundreds, perhaps thousands, of people were suddenly trapped by the storm surge. They were left not only trapped—they were struggling for their lives.

Floodwaters poured rapidly into the low-lying neighborhoods of the Lower and Upper Ninth Wards, and

Mississippi

At a press conference, Governor Haley Barbour announced, "It came in to Mississippi like a ton of bricks. It's a terrible storm. There are structures after structures that survived Camille with minor damage that are not there any more. There were 10- and 20-block areas where there was nothing—not one home standing."[2]

East New Orleans. Within minutes, even seconds, water swirled around houses. The flood seeped in through every gap, covering floors, then continuing to rise. As deep as it was outside, that is how high the water rose indoors. And it quickly crept to first-floor ceilings.

People had to find higher ground—fast. A few managed to get outside before their houses filled

Flooding

Many residents who rode out Katrina on New Orleans' west side thought they had escaped serious damage once the storm passed. But not long after, they looked out their windows in horror as water quietly rose up around them. "The hurricane was scary. All the tree branches fell, but the building stood," said Scott Radish. "I thought I was doing good. Then I noticed my Jeep was underwater."[3] According to his wife, Kyle, water rose up the side of the house, one brick every 20 minutes.

up completely. In heavy rains and sheer terror, people climbed up anything they could get their hands on as the rising water lifted them higher, even up to their rooftops. Some clung to floating objects, such as refrigerators or dressers, and had to paddle to nearby buildings. But many did not get out. They had no choice but to climb into their darkened attics, crouching in rooms with no windows and little ventilation. Still, the water rose.

Not knowing if the flood would keep rising, people tore at their roofs from the inside. They used anything they could find—hammers, crowbars, broom handles, knives—to break through. For some it took hours to escape, but they eventually made it out. Others, many elderly, could only pound on their walls and scream for help.

Their voices were heard by rescuers and bystanders thoughout Monday afternoon. As one reporter said:

> From the bridge, you could see people on their roofs and, more hauntingly, hear them shouting for help. Their screams echoed through the wet air and seemed to bounce off the floodwaters. ... It appeared every home had people trapped inside.[4]

RESCUE

Risking their own lives, rescuers had set out even before the storm had passed. The Coast Guard, police and fire teams, even neighborhood residents, used any watercraft available to search the city's flooded east side. Rescuers shuttled among submerged homes, listening for shouts from within. They cut through rooftops and used rope harnesses to pull people out.

As winds settled and evening approached, Coast Guard helicopters roared into action. They, too, went from house to house, picking up residents, many of whom had been stranded for more than a dozen hours. Between helicopters and boats, the task went on into the night. Over and over, people were picked up and carried to dry land. Hundreds of people were saved.

The day was filled with heroism. Residents went in search of their elderly neighbors, sometimes diving underwater and swimming through submerged windows to pull a terrified friend to safety. Others just turned to any stranger in need.

Yet, many did not survive. An enormous area of the city, as well as St. Bernard and Plaquemines parishes, was caught in a horrible flood. For all the people who escaped, there may have been hundreds more who did not. But in the frantic rush to save the living, rescuers could not stop. The dead would have to wait.

Alabama

Mobile, Alabama, lay on the eastern edge of Katrina's hurricane strength. There, an 11-foot (3 m) storm surge crashed into the city. Afterward, much of downtown Mobile lay under eight feet (2.5 m) of water. The storm pushed the Chemul, a 13,000-ton oil rig, out of dry dock and up the Mobile River. It eventually stopped when it crashed into the Cochrane-Africatown USA Bridge, about 1 mile (1.6 km) upstream.

Taking Refuge from the Flood

Meanwhile, throughout the city, thousands of residents raced toward higher ground. With water slowly rising on all sides, people trudged toward the Superdome, hoping to find safety and shelter.

Surrounded by three feet (1 m) of water, the building was already a scene of chaos. The lights ran

Residents are rescued by helicopter from the floodwaters of Hurricane Katrina.

on a handful of emergency generators. The air conditioning had gone out and the temperature was above 90 degrees Fahrenheit (32 °C). By midday, the plumbing had broken down and toilets failed to work. With the building's population at 26,000 and only 500 soldiers on hand, the National Guard was barely able to keep order.

Though the Ernest N. Memorial Convention Center was not originally planned for use as a shelter, people had streamed into the building since before the storm on Sunday night. Approximately 2,000 people rode out the storm at the Convention Center. By Wednesday, August 31, just two days after Katrina hit New Orleans, that number would rise to 20,000.

New Orleans residents make their way through
floodwaters toward higher ground.

Helicopters drop sandbags to fill the broken section of a levee.

NEW ORLEANS CRUMBLES

Eighty percent of New Orleans was flooded. Efforts to plug the breach in the 17th Street Canal had gone on all night. Military helicopters dropped giant sandbags into the gaping hole. The effort barely made a dent. The breach was deep and long. Water kept coming as the high water levels in Lake Pontchartrain emptied into the city. As the day wore on, sandbags fell into short supply, helicopters had to be diverted for rescue missions, and the hole just kept swallowing everything the engineers dumped into it. The patching process took several more days of round-the-clock work to complete. Until then, water continued to flow.

Did the Levees Fail?

First, large amounts of water poured over the top of the levee walls. That water crashed to the base of the levee, softening the foundation. In many cases, the water was so powerful, it even dug out the ground at the wall's base. With the foundation weakened, the huge amounts of water would simply push the levee walls over. Breaches happened at older levees as well as ones that had been recently reinforced.

RESCUE IN CHAOS

Despite dire predictions, those in charge of responding were ill-equipped to handle the sheer size of the catastrophe. There were not enough rescuers. There were not enough boats, trucks, and other equipment. There was not enough medical help. There was not enough of anything people needed on the spot.

The communication breakdowns caused gridlock between different rescue units. The extent of damage was far from clear. Few knew where the worst problems were. National Guard troops had to follow reporters, who relayed messages by cell phone, to devastated areas.

All across the city, crowds waited on tiny islands of dry land for trucks to evacuate them to a safer place. Because of devastated roads, the trucks were slow in coming, or did not come at all.

FEMA Director Michael Brown

Before becoming head of the Federal Emergency Management Agency (FEMA), Michael Brown had virtually no experience running emergency relief operations. He joined the agency as an attorney but was soon made a deputy director. When Joseph Allbaugh left the director job, President Bush promoted Brown to lead the agency.

Brown can be credited for warning the President and the Department of Homeland Security before the storm that Katrina could be catastrophic for New Orleans. His response in the aftermath, however, became a national issue. Brown was criticized for seeming uninformed about the tragedy in the streets. Meanwhile, many felt FEMA's response to the situation was inadequate. When questions started to flare, Brown criticized local leaders. He blamed Governor Blanco and Mayor Nagin, saying, "In Katrina, I was never able to establish a unified command structure because Louisiana was so dysfunctional and so overwhelmed."[1]

On September 9, Department of Homeland Security secretary Michael Chertoff removed Brown from his leadership of FEMA's Katrina relief effort. Three days later, under intense pressure and public outcry, Brown resigned.

In the days that followed, rescuers scrambled to assist those in need. But progress could not be made fast enough to satisfy the thousands of evacuees who now depended on federal relief.

A LACK OF RESPONSE

Local officials were overwhelmed. Mayor Nagin and his staff, first caught in the storm's rampage at the Hyatt Regency hotel, were later stuck at City Hall as their satellite phones steadily ran out of power. Fire units were drawn off vital rescue missions to handle fires breaking out across the city. Police officers struggled to keep the search-and-rescue process going, which drew them away from growing troubles in the streets.

Looking for Federal Aid

Hopeful for federal help, city and state leaders turned to President Bush, the Department of Homeland Security, and FEMA. Just hours after the storm, Governor Blanco called President Bush saying, "Mr. President, we need your help. We need everything you've got."[2]

The city turned to the state. Governor Blanco sent for more National Guard troops. She asked fellow governors for more first responders and closed New Orleans to returning residents until the city could be declared safe again. She went to the Superdome to survey the situation there. But the state, too, lacked the full resources to deal with this problem. This was a disaster of extraordinary proportions. Local and state responders struggled to meet the needs of this ever-worsening situation.

On the morning Katrina struck, FEMA director Michael Brown warned the president about the severity of the storm. Brown additionally called for 1,000 more FEMA employees to head for New Orleans.

By 11:13 a.m., a report arrived at the White House that levees inside New Orleans had breached and the city was flooding. Later, FEMA representatives and other officials reported conflicting news on the storm. Communication between federal agencies had already broken down. Unfortunately, the cost was precious hours lost.

That evening, in New Orleans, a FEMA representative arrived at Mayor Nagin's office. He had surveyed the city and was alarmed by the extensive flooding and damage. He was having trouble reaching his superiors in Washington. When he finally got through, he was heard saying over and over, "You don't understand. You don't understand."[3]

Department of Homeland Security secretary Michael Chertoff claimed to believe the 17th Street Canal breach did not occur until the next day. In his assessment, he stated,

> It was on Tuesday that the levee—may have been overnight Monday to Tuesday—that the levee started to break. And it was midday Tuesday that I became aware of the fact that there was no possibility of plugging the gap and that essentially the lake was going to start to drain into the city.[4]

LOOKING FOR RELIEF

While the government stumbled, New Orleanians escaped from their flooded homes. They waded through polluted floodwaters hoping to find relief.

The scene at the Superdome was getting worse. The number of displaced persons had swollen to 26,000. Three feet (1 m) of water surrounded the building and a crack in the structure flooded one of the generators.

The scene at the convention center was just as bad. Upwards of 20,000 people came to the building believing they would find help. But the building had never been intended as a shelter. There was no preparation: no food, no water, not even guardsmen or police to maintain order. People gathered and waited, thinking help would arrive. In the chaos, many rescuers did not even know anyone was there. Four people died inside.

Still, four days after the storm, Brown said on the ABC news program *Nightline* that he only

Disorder at the Superdome

At one point, the bathrooms at the Superdome had stopped working and toilets backed up and overflowed, filling the 19-acre structure with a sickening stench. With no bathrooms to use, people had no choice but to find another spot to go to the bathroom, making the situation even worse. Tempers matched the rising temperatures inside.

Hospital Ship

For days after Katrina hit, the U.S.S. Bataan sat off the Louisiana coast waiting for orders. The navy hospital ship offered 6 operating rooms and beds for 600 patients.

learned of the troubles just that evening. Anchor Ted Koppel replied, "Don't you guys watch television? Don't you guys listen to the radio?"[5]

The Superdome and convention center became focal points of national outrage and shame. Television coverage displayed a stream of horrible images while rumors ran wild of gangs, murder, and rape. The desperate refugees were losing hope that help would ever arrive. After three days at the convention center, Tony Cash said,

> It was as if all of us were already pronounced dead. As if somebody already had the body bags. Wasn't nobody coming to get us.[6]

New Orleans residents get on buses on September 1. Residents relocated across the country while New Orleans was cleared and readied for their return.

Residents stranded in New Orleans resorted to stealing food.

A City in Turmoil

*I*n the long, hot days that followed, people in New Orleans wondered when their nightmare would end. Help arrived, but it barely scratched the surface of the disaster. While rescuers worked, the few areas of the city that remained dry were left virtually without aid or order.

LAWLESS STREETS

At the convention center and the Superdome, people cowered in corners, argued over slivers of personal space, begged for help, and cried for their losses. Many others wandered the streets looking for shelter, their homes swallowed under the flood. Food, water, and help were all in short supply. As one uncertain hour led to the next, fear and desperation mixed with resentment and rage.

Chaos

"We need additional troops, food, water," said Joseph Matthews, head of New Orleans' Office of Emergency Preparedness, "and we need personnel, law enforcement. This has turned into a situation where the city is being run by thugs."[1] Katrina had stirred up a new kind of chaos.

Out of the chaos, criminals emerged. Even in the first hours after the storm, reports arrived of looting— people breaking into buildings and stealing whatever they could find. In downtown New Orleans, the area east of the Superdome remained mostly clear of floodwaters. Journalists reported hearing gunshots there as early as Monday night. With nearly every police officer and other first responders tied up in rescue efforts, the streets were open to crime.

Soon, refugees of the storm joined the looting out of desperation. Many had been without food or water since the storm. They followed gangs into supermarkets, pharmacies, and convenience stores, making meals from whatever they could find. With no sign of help on the way, many angrily believed they had no choice but to find whatever they could—wherever they could. They took survival into their own hands.

By Wednesday night, August 31, Mayor Nagin called as many police officers as he could off rescue missions and back into the streets. But by then, the looting was widespread. Reports even came in of police officers joining the looting.

In frustration, Governor Blanco requested 40,000 National Guard troops be sent to

Where Were the Police?

One of the most frustrating stories to come out of the aftermath of Katrina was that a huge portion of the New Orleans police force fled during the storm, leaving the city without protection. At the time, there were reports that more than 500 officers—nearly a third of the entire force—had walked off their posts. Just a few days after the storm, New Orleans Police Superintendent Eddie Compass called the missing officers cowards. But within a few weeks, more accurate totals counted that 249 officers had gone missing—some were stranded on their rooftops like thousands of other city residents.

In truth, during the storm and in the first days after, New Orleans police performed valiantly. They worked around the clock to rescue thousands, with little outside help. Captain Jeff Wynn described the pace:

"I'm talking about getting a bunch of tag guys out of a boat. Going over and looking at a target. Taking down that target. Getting back in that boat. And going another two blocks over. Cutting a rooftop open and getting the family out. It just never stopped."[2]

New Orleans. A contingent of
Arkansas troops, which had just
returned from the war in Iraq, were
among the first to arrive. Governor
Blanco angrily announced to looters,
"They have M-16s and they are locked
and loaded. I have one message for
these hoodlums. These troops know
how to shoot and kill, and they are
more than willing to do so if
necessary."[3]

Snipers?

Despite reports of rescue helicopters being fired upon by snipers, such rumors were never officially confirmed.

By that time, an image of a lawless city had already
shocked the nation. Television footage showed burning
buildings, looted and vandalized stores, and people
in the streets with shopping carts full of stolen stereos
or athletic shoes. Against this ugly backdrop, the
displaced and the criminals began to look the same.
New Orleans showed a frightening, dark side.

Stalled Rescue

Like the looting, the slow pace of rescue was another
image of chaos in New Orleans. The Superdome was
turning into a disaster: it was filthy, hot, and reeking
of human waste. The scene was worse at the convention
center, where people chanted, "Help, help!" as

cameramen surveyed the scene. Frantic mobs rushed at helicopters trying to deliver aid. The refugees at both locations had to be evacuated. Mayor Nagin called for more help on September 1:

> This is a desperate SOS. Right now we are out of resources at the convention center and don't anticipate enough buses. We need buses. Currently the convention center is unsanitary and unsafe and we're running out of supplies.[4]

Contaminated Water

When the floodwater swallowed up homes, businesses, and industrial facilities, it also swallowed countless gallons of spilled toxic chemicals. The flooding also disrupted the city's water system, forcing tons of raw sewage into the mix. In many spots, natural gas seeped from broken lines up through the water, sometimes catching fire at the surface. The result was a terrible stew of filthy, smelly, unhealthy water. Unfortunately, thousands had to wade through it as they fled their homes. At least five people later died from bacterial infections believed to be caused by exposure to the water.

The city of Houston, Texas, agreed to provide relief shelter for tens of thousands of refugees. It opened the Astrodome, a sports facility very much like the Superdome. But the horrible scenes in New Orleans continued while FEMA struggled to move buses into the city. Evacuees could only wait in the sweltering heat. Some had been there since August 27. Anger filled the air. "We're just a bunch of rats," said Earle Young as he stood in line for a bus. "That's how they've been

Evacuees wait for aid at the crowded Convention Center in New Orleans.

treating us."[5] Terry Ebbert, director of Homeland Security in New Orleans, said the slow evacuation had become a dangerous situation.

In other parts of the city, hundreds of people gathered under the shade of highway overpasses,

Slow Response

Jefferson Parish president Aaron Broussard was furious over the slow pace of federal response. On national television, he said, "We have been abandoned by our own country. Hurricane Katrina will go down in history as one of the worst storms ever to hit an American coast, but the aftermath of Hurricane Katrina will go down as one of the worst abandonments of Americans on American soil ever in U.S. history. ... It's not just Katrina that caused all these deaths in New Orleans here. Bureaucracy has committed murder here in the greater New Orleans area, and bureaucracy has to stand trial before Congress now."[6]

wondering when—or if—relief trucks would arrive. At hospitals across New Orleans, emergency generators began running out of fuel. More than 1,600 patients and at least 8,000 doctors, nurses, and other staff awaited evacuation.

Outside the convention center, the dead body of 91-year-old Booker Harris sat in a lawn chair, wrapped in a yellow quilt. While the city boiled in troubles, his body sat untouched for another two days. Harris was one of dozens of the dead in plain sight.

No one knew just how many people had been killed, but fears ran high. Mayor Nagin said on September 1, "We know there is a significant number of dead bodies in the water." He estimated the death toll as, "Minimum, hundreds. Most likely, thousands."[7] A few days later, he raised his prediction to an astounding 10,000.

Too Few Answers

As New Orleans slipped deeper into its hellish state, outraged leaders in Louisiana furiously attacked the federal government for its slow and confused response. "This is a national emergency. This is a national disgrace," said Ebbert. He angrily declared that FEMA "has been here three days, yet there is no command and control. We can send massive amounts of aid to tsunami victims, but we can't bail out the city of New Orleans."[8]

FEMA director Michael Brown and Homeland Security chief Michael Chertoff faced harsh criticism for the reaction to the disaster. Mayor Nagin declared that the situation in New Orleans had become "the biggest ... crisis in the history of this country." He denounced federal officials, saying they "don't have a clue what's going on down here. There is nothing happening. And they're feeding the public a line of bull, and they're spinning."[9]

President Bush was criticized for not taking the tragic situation seriously enough. Many said he failed to back up his words with swift action and to lead in the crisis. At first, Bush ignored the criticism. Later, he admitted mistakes had been made. Bush said,

Katrina exposed serious problems in our response capability at all levels of government and to the extent the federal government didn't fully do its job right, I take responsibility.[10]

EMPTYING NEW ORLEANS

The last refugees left the Superdome and the convention center on Sunday, September 4, nearly one week after Katrina came and went. Over the previous several days, more than 42,000 people had been evacuated from the city.

With conditions as bad as they were, Mayor Nagin declared a mandatory evacuation of New Orleans. He said the city was unsafe and unhealthy and estimated it would take two to three months before residents could return. The mayor authorized National Guard troops to remove anyone who resisted evacuation. New Orleans had to be emptied of its people.

Mayor Nagin addresses reporters September 15, 2005,
to discuss the rebuilding of New Orleans.

Chapter 9

Animals wander the deserted streets of New Orleans.

LOSS AND RECOVERY

Over 100,000 people fled New Orleans before Katrina struck. Now, one week into the aftermath, with 80 percent of the city underwater and the other 20 percent shut down, the last New Orleanians had to leave.

Patrols of police, National Guard troops, and other rescuers circulated on foot and in boats. Some holdouts were finally ready to go. They locked their doors and hoped for the best. But others still refused. New Orleans was their home, and the house they lived in was all they had. In a few neighborhoods, locals banded together to defy the order. They shared food and bottled water, began clearing debris from their yards, and carried weapons to ward off looters. Delia Labarre told a reporter, "My ancestors were original colonists of the city, and they didn't tuck their tail between their legs and run."[1] Still, everyone had to go.

Relocating

To help Americans connect with displaced refugees, Serena Howard of Fayetteville, Arkansas, started a Web site called openyourhome.com. Her site, along with others like it, helped thousands of refugees all across the United States find places to stay.

WITHOUT A HOME

But where did the people of New Orleans go—the hundreds of thousands who were left without their city, without their homes?

By the night of Sunday, September 4, Texas governor Rick Perry announced that his state had taken in nearly 250,000 refugees. In Houston, the Astrodome filled to capacity within 24 hours. City

Hurricane Katrina refugees are temporarily housed in Houston's Astrodome.

officials opened three more large buildings. In all, 50,000 people found safety in the makeshift shelters. They also found showers and clean towels, working bathrooms, blankets and cots, and the first hot meal some had seen in a week. Dallas took in more than 25,000 refugees, as did San Antonio.

Doors opened all across the country. The Red Cross, the organization taking a lead in the relief effort, opened nearly 500 shelters in 12 states. Arkansas took in 70,000 refugees. Thousands of other evacuees from Mississippi and Alabama made their way to shelters in Tennessee, Kentucky, and Georgia. In total, an estimated 1.3 million people fled the region.

In the chaos after the storm, many families were separated. Then, the evacuation process carried people thousands of miles apart. Many families would not reconnect for weeks, some not knowing if their loved ones had survived the storm. The walls of evacuation centers and shelters were covered with letters and photographs from people looking for missing friends and relatives.

Stranded

Natrena Lewis was stranded on a rooftop with her two boys, Telly, age five, and Ty'iyr, 22 months. A helicopter airlifted Ty'iyr but didn't have enough room for his mother and brother. A few days later, Natrena and Telly were rescued and evacuated to Houston. But she did not know where Ty'iyr had been taken. Finally, days later, thanks to a relative in the Air Force, Ty'iyr was found in a hospital—in Atlanta, Georgia, more than 2,000 miles (3,200 km) away.

An Outpouring of Aid

Americans across the nation opened their homes to the incredible wave of refugees. Families as far away as

Washington, Minnesota, and Maine took in the stranded and homeless. Thousands of families found the same hospitality in every part of the country. Schools expanded their classrooms and hired displaced teachers from Mississippi and Louisiana.

The aid came in other ways, too. Tens of millions of Americans generously opened their wallets to the relief effort. Within a week after Katrina struck, over half a billion dollars poured in. No amount that great had ever been raised in such a short time. A vast percentage came from individual donations. The giving reflected the deep sense

Taking Responsibility

During a brief tour through the ruins of New Orleans, a reporter asked President Bush about the slow pace of the federal effort. He responded, "Look, there will be plenty of time to play the blame game."[2]

He was right. The pitch of anger and blame had already gone on for days and showed no signs of stopping. Accusations spread to cries of racism, pointing out that the majority of victims caught in the aftermath of Katrina were poor and African American. Local officials denounced FEMA and the President for not caring enough.

Other members of Congress declared the response a failure of leadership, a case of incompetence and mismanagement. Calls came for FEMA director Michael Brown and even Homeland Security secretary Michael Chertoff to resign. Congress began an almost immediate investigation.

Dr. Walter Maestri, Director of Emergency Operations for Jefferson Parish, said, "We're all angry, including me, because promises made were not promises kept. We were told we would be on our own for 48 hours and then the cavalry would arrive, but it didn't. Our citizens feel a breach of trust. ... A lot of our people feel cheated."[3]

of anguish and connection many Americans felt for the struggling survivors.

Collection jars appeared on store counters. Children organized donations at their schools and adults gathered money in their workplaces. Churches and service organizations called on their members and friends to give. And give they did. The flow of dollars amazed even the Red Cross. Businesses also showed their strength. By the end of the month, the Red Cross reported the donation total had reached nearly $1 billion.

Bacteria

Microbiologists tested the flood waters in the Lower Ninth Ward and found them to be 45,000 times more contaminated than what is considered safe for swimming. Paul Pearce reported, "In terms of total microorganisms in floodwater, this is about as bad as it can get."[4]

Back in New Orleans, and across the crippled region, hundreds of volunteers arrived to help in any way they could. Police, fire crews, and countless volunteers moved in, setting up tent villages. Hospitals around the country organized whole teams of medical staff and supplies. Trucks loaded with food, water, and clothing made their way to the thousands of refugees living in emergency shelters.

Donations

A fund set up by former presidents George H. W. Bush and Bill Clinton raised more than $1 million within 24 hours through online donations.

DRYING OUT, DIGGING OUT

The Army Corps of Engineers worked around the clock to repair New Orleans' levee breaches and restore the pumps to full capacity. More than 1,500 corps members arrived after the storm. Army Blackhawk and Chinook helicopters continually dropped 7,000 pound (3,000 kg) bags of sand into the breaches. On Sunday afternoon, September 4, the Corps announced they had closed the breach at the 17th Street Canal. They could pump water full force back into Lake Pontchartrain without it circling right back into the city. On September 6, they had closed the smaller breach at the London Avenue Canal. The process of pumping water out of New Orleans was slow. But the process quickened each day as more equipment arrived from other states and repaired pumps went back online.

The flood water slowly receded. But millions of cubic feet of mud would remain, filled with bacteria, heavy metals, and oil. Police and military teams set up blockades at the city's edges to keep people out. Remarkably, the drying out process was completed by October 2, barely a month after Katrina struck.

Theador Hunter, left, and his daughter, Tracy, are reunited in Houston after being separated during Hurricane Katrina.

Chapter 10

Two sisters return to New Orleans to find their home damaged from the flooding.

THE ROAD AHEAD

As days turned to weeks, the 1.3 million people evacuated from the Gulf Coast wondered when they could return to their homes—or even if they had homes to return to. Many held out hope that they would be able to return to the city and rebuild their homes and lives as they once were, in the city they loved. They waited for word that it was safe to return to the city.

Others, feeling exhausted and depressed, said they would never return. Orelius Caldwell found new hope in Little Rock, Arkansas: "I went from New Orleans, where I had nothing, to a place where I have something."[1]

Water removal in New Orleans went quickly. But the city and most of the region lay under a layer of mud, downed trees and power lines, and damaged buildings. Cleanup would take months. Millions of cubic yards of debris had to be removed. Roads and bridges needed repair. So did electricity, clean water, and gas lines. That meant countless hours of work replacing damaged equipment, house after house. Houses submerged in the flood would have to be cleared of garbage, unhealthy molds, and bacteria. Hundreds of homes had to be gutted down to their exterior frames. The recovery process went on, day by day. By November 2005, a few thousand residents were living in New

New Life

Denita Prout and her fiancé, Lance Turner, found shelter in Dallas, Texas. They said they would not go back to their apartment in Plaquemines Parish. Turner said, "Whatever we had before is underwater. Our path took us here. We will try to make it here."[2]

Orleans again. But they had come back to a city only partly alive—death still held a grip.

Ollie Robinson first returned to clean up her home after seven months away. She said,

> It's like coming back to something that has been bombed. No one is here. And to see how everything had been stirred around—especially around here—all the furniture had been moved around and twisted around, a deep freezer blocking the door. You can't open your doors. It stinks. You have got rats. It is just a mess. And we are trying to just start over.[3]

Still, she remained hopeful that her home—and her city—would come to life again.

CONTINUED PROBLEMS WITH FEDERAL RELIEF

More than one year after the storm, FEMA continued to stir anger. Government aid commitments of $110 billion slowly trickled back into the region. In one $7.5 billion-dollar program, only 87 people had received funds—out of 89,403 applications. Barely half the trailers designated for people in New Orleans had been delivered and many did not fully work. Recovery

Recovery

Weeks after Katrina, President Bush put it simply and accurately: "This recovery will take years."[4]

A hurricane survivor wipes away tears after sifting through the remains of her house.

checks to residents were slow in coming and some had been cut off for no reason. Donna Sanford managed a $3 billion Mississippi program to support under-insured homeowners. More than a year into the relief effort, she had been authorized to give checks to less than half of those in need.

> *If you had asked me in April if I would be sitting here in December and I would only have 7,000 checks out, I would have laughed in your face. It just sounded so simple.*[5]

Many area residents felt the same despair. David Lain had escaped to Texas after Katrina then quickly headed back to his hometown of Long Beach, Mississippi. A year later he was still living in a trailer parked on his property. He said:

If you would have told me a year ago that we were still going to be in this situation, I would have gone back to Texas. I wouldn't have gone through this.[6]

SCATTERED SIGNS OF RECOVERY

Despite the overwhelming scale, the slow process, and the struggle to get a grip on relief efforts, hope remained that the battered region would get back on

---

Hurricane Rita

Less than three weeks after Hurricane Katrina, New Orleans was threatened again by a major hurricane. On September 18, 2005, Tropical Storm Rita had developed east of Florida and followed nearly the same path as Katrina. By September 21, Rita had swollen into a Category 3 hurricane, then jumped to a Category 5 only 14 hours later.

The Army Corps of Engineers in New Orleans warned that the weakened levees in the city might not be able to withstand another major blow. Only a few days before, Mayor Nagin had allowed a few citizens back into the city. Now he had to order another mandatory evacuation.

When Rita appeared headed for Houston, Texas, Governor Rick Perry called for evacuations of the region. More than 2.5 million people fled the coastal area, from south of Houston to the central Louisiana coast. The tens of thousands of Katrina refugees still taking shelter in the Houston Astrodome and other centers in the area now had to move a second time.

Rita struck as a Category 3 storm on Saturday, September 24. Tropical storm winds reached New Orleans and caused several inches of rain, including some minor street flooding.

its feet. The outpouring of support continued from across the nation and signs of rebuilding appeared in the barren landscape.

In New Orleans' residential neighborhoods, the pace of recovery varied—mostly by income. Middle and upper class areas were well into rebuilding by the spring of 2006. New and refurbished homes stood along clean, resurfaced streets. Landscapers were hard at work replacing grass, trees, and shrubs. But in some of the poorest sections of New Orleans, little had changed after even a year. The Lower Ninth Ward, where more than 14,000 people had once lived, remained abandoned. The flood had damaged 1,300 buildings, yet the city had issued only four permits to rebuild. Houses stood empty, reeking of mold. Debris lay in the streets, and the water system still was not up and running. Before Katrina, a bustling New Orleans boasted more than 400,000 residents. A year later, fewer than half had returned.

Deserted

One of the first to return to New Orleans after the hurricane, Pat Breaux, a cardiologist living near Lake Pontchartrain said, "It's spooky out there. There's no life."[7]

Many homes were damaged beyond repair.

KATRINA'S LEGACY

Hurricane Katrina will be remembered for generations. It was, by far, the most destructive hurricane ever to strike the United States.

Weeks after the storm, cleanup crews continued to find bodies among the wreckage. The final death toll reached 1,833. That number includes 1,577 in Louisiana, most in New Orleans. In Mississippi, deaths numbered 238. Another 14 people died in Florida, along with two in Alabama, and two in Georgia.

Damage costs topped $100 billion, far greater than any other natural disaster in U.S. history. Cleanup alone rose to more than $1 billion. A year after the storm, estimates for rebuilding New Orleans' levees jumped to over $10 billion.

More than 850,000 homes were damaged by the storm, including 70 percent of New Orleans' houses. Katrina also forced 200,000 businesses to close throughout the coastal region. Some never reopened. The damage to the Gulf Coast's economy meant that many people returned to find they had not only lost their homes, they were also out of work. Every town damaged by Katrina faces a cloud of uncertainties.

THE FUTURE

Hurricane Katrina taught the nation many lessons. It generated serious debate and reflection. Communication, evacuation procedures, and warning systems will all change. Relief efforts, collaboration, and government structures will change too. Because of these changes, the United States should be much better prepared for the next major emergency.

Atlantic Hurricane Season of 2005

In terms of overall damage, Hurricane Katrina was by far the most destructive storm ever to hit the United States. The Atlantic Hurricane Season of 2005 was the most active storm season in 154 years of record keeping. A record 28 named storms formed, including 15 hurricanes, the most in a single season.

But Katrina also raised certain warnings for which there may never be solutions. While New Orleans rebuilds, it will continue to sink below sea level. The shoals and beaches along the Louisiana coast will continue to recede. No matter how dire the warnings, or prepared the government is, there will be people unable or unwilling to heed the evacuation call.

Most importantly of all, the hurricanes will come again. Some meteorologists say the storms will be larger and more powerful than ever. And we know that another "Big One" will strike. It is not a matter of if but when.

The water begins to drain from the Lower Ninth Ward, revealing areas of heavy, dried mud.

TIMELINE

August 23, 2005	August 24, 2005	August 25, 2005
Tropical Depression 12 forms over the southeastern Bahamas.	The National Hurricane Center upgrades Tropical Depression 12 to Tropical Storm Katrina.	Tropical Storm Katrina is upgraded to Hurricane Katrina and makes landfall near Miami, Florida.

August 29, 2005	August 30, 2005	August 31, 2005
Hurricane Katrina makes landfall at Buras, Louisiana and the Louisiana/Mississippi border. Levees protecting New Orleans are breached.	Eighty percent of New Orleans is flooded. Rescue operations continue with hundreds of Coast Guard, National Guard, and local first responders.	Mayor Nagin orders New Orleans police off search and rescue duties, in order to return to city streets to control the looting.

August 26, 2005

Governor Blanco declares a state of emergency.

August 27, 2005

Hurricane Katrina is upgraded to Category 3. A state of emergency is declared for Mississippi and New Orleans.

August 28, 2005

Hurricane Katrina is upgraded to a Category 5 hurricane. Mayor Nagin orders a mandatory evacuation of New Orleans. The Superdome becomes a "refuge of last resort."

September 1, 2005

Governor Blanco calls for 40,000 National Guard troops to support the rescue and security operation in New Orleans.

September 2, 2005

Evacuation continues at the Superdome, while more survivors arrive looking for aid. President Bush arrives to tour New Orleans.

September 3, 2005

Evacuation of the 20,000 people at the convention center is underway.

TIMELINE

September 4, 2005

The last refugees are evacuated from the Superdome and convention center. The Army Corps of Engineers closes the breach in the 17th Street Canal.

September 5, 2005

The Army Corps of Engineers closes the London Avenue Canal breeches. They begin pumping water out of New Orleans.

September 21, 2005

Hurricane Rita jumps from a Category 3 hurricane to Category 5. Millions evacuate Houston and the coastline along Texas and western Louisiana.

September 24, 2005

Hurricane Rita strikes along the coast at the Texas/Louisiana border as a Category 3 hurricane. Heavy rains fall over New Orleans causing some minor flooding.

September 12, 2005

Michael Brown resigns as director of FEMA.

September 19, 2005

The National Weather Service warns that Tropical Storm Rita is headed into the Gulf of Mexico and may make landfall near New Orleans.

2007

Residents return to New Orleans. Many still await zoning decisions on rebuilding.

ESSENTIAL FACTS

DATE OF EVENT

August 29, 2005, to September 5, 2005, Hurricane Katrina makes landfall at Buras, Louisiana.

PLACE OF EVENT

New Orleans, Louisiana and other states bordering the Gulf of Mexico, especially Mississippi, Florida, and Georgia.

KEY PLAYERS

❖ Ray Nagin, New Orleans Mayor

❖ Michael Brown, FEMA director

❖ Kathleen Blanco, Louisiana Governor

❖ George W. Bush, United States President

HIGHLIGHTS OF EVENT

❖ A storm forms in the Bahamas on August 23, 2005, and becomes a Category 5 hurricane by August 28.

❖ Mayor Nagin orders the evacuation of New Orleans, Louisiana, and opens the Superdome as a refuge to those unable to leave the city.

❖ Michael Brown resigns as director of FEMA.

❖ Levees are repaired and flood waters are pumped out of the city.

❖ Residents are allowed to return and begin rebuilding.

QUOTE

"Katrina exposed serious problems in our response capability at all levels of government and to the extent the federal government didn't fully do its job right, I take responsibility." — *George W. Bush*

"It's like coming back to something that has been bombed. No one is here. … You can't open your doors. It stinks. You have got rats. It is just a mess. And we are trying to just start over." —*Ollie Robinson, New Orleans resident*

ADDITIONAL RESOURCES

SELECT BIBLIOGRAPHY

Hurricane Katrina Special Report
www.cnn.com/SPECIALS/2005/katrina/

Knauer, Kelly, ed. *Hurricane Katrina: The Storm That Changed America*. New York: Time Books, 2005.

The National Hurricane Center
www.nhc.noaa.gov/

FURTHER READING

Miller, Debra A. *Hurricane Katrina: Devastation on the Gulf Coast*. San Diego, CA: Lucent Books, 2006.

Rodger, Ellen. *Hurricane Katrina*. New York: Crabtree, 2006.

Torres, John. *Hurricane Katrina and the Devastation of New Orleans*. Hockessin, DE: Mitchell Lane Publishers, 2006.

Web Links

To learn more about Hurricane Katrina, visit ABDO Publishing Company on the World Wide Web at **www.abdopublishing.com**. Web sites about Hurricane Katrina are featured on our Book Links page. These links are routinely monitored and updated to provide the most current information available.

Places to Visit

New Orleans Convention and Visitors Bureau
2020 Charles Avenue, New Orleans, LA 70130
1-800-672-6124
www.neworleanscvb.com
The visitor center for New Orleans can direct visitors to entertainment, dining, and cultural activities in New Orleans.

Mississippi Gulf Coast Convention and Visitors Bureau
135 Courthouse Road, Biloxi, MS 39507
601-896-6699
www.gulfcoast.org
Visitors to the Mississippi Gulf Coast can enjoy the beaches and historic sites in the area.

New Orleans Area Habitat for Humanity
7100 St. Charles Avenue, New Orleans, LA 70118
504-861-2077
www.habitat-nola.org
The New Orleans Area Habitat for Humanity welcomes volunteers who wish to help rebuild homes in New Orleans and the surrounding area.

Glossary

breach
>   To break through a wall or barrier.

cyclone
>   A tropical cyclone that forms over the Indian Ocean.

delta
>   Triangular sediment deposited at the mouth of a river.

deluge
>   A severe flood.

Department of Homeland Security
>   The federal agency in charge of protecting the United States from potential disasters or reacting to disasters should they occur.

erosion
>   The gradual wearing away of rock, soil, or beach through the action of wind and/or water.

eye
>   The open, circular area in the center of a tropical cyclone. Winds are light and calm.

eye wall
>   The band of clouds immediately surrounding the eye of the tropical cyclone. Winds are strongest at this edge and rainfall his heaviest.

FEMA
>   Federal Emergency Management Agency. The federal agency in charge of disaster relief.

flood
>   Water appearing in a usually dry area of land. A flood can be caused by high rains, or rising water in the area.

landfall
The point where the eye of a hurricane first makes contact with land.

levee
A wall built to hold back water. A levee can be made of soil and rocks or built of construction materials such as concrete.

looting
The act of stealing property from a business or home in the aftermath of a natural disaster or human conflict.

major hurricane
A hurricane classified as Category 3 or higher, having sustained winds of 111 miles per hour (178 km/h) or higher.

maximum sustained winds
The maximum wind speed a tropical cyclone generates lasting for a minute or more.

storm surge
The swell of sea water pushed ahead by a storm. A storm surge strikes land ahead of a tropical cyclone's landfall.

subsidence
The gradual sinking of an area.

tropical cyclone
A storm system forming over tropical or sub-tropical waters that develops into a spiral shape with strong sustained winds— at least 74 miles per hour (119 km/h).

typhoon
A tropical cyclone that forms over the Pacific Ocean.

Source Notes

Chapter 1. The Approaching Storm
1. "Hurricane Katrina Advisory Number 17." National Oceanic and Atmospheric Administration, 27 Aug. 2005. NHC.NOAA.GOV, 18 Oct. 2006 <http://www.nhc.noaa.gov/archive/2005/pub/al122005.public.019.shtml>.

Chapter 2. A Delicate Balance
1. Kelly Knauer. ed. *Hurricane Katrina: The Storm that Changed America*. New York: Time Books, 2005. vi.

2. Mark Fischetti. "Drowning New Orleans." *Scientific American*. Oct. 2001. Scientific American.com. 12 Oct. 2006 <http://www.sciam.com/article.cfm?articleID=00060286-CB58-1315-8B5883414B7F0000&pageNumber=2&catID=2>.

3. Ann Carrns and Betsy McKay. "Levees May be Key to New Orleans Survival." *The Post-Gazette*. 31 Aug. 2005. Post-Gazette.com. 3 Nov. 2006 <http://www.post-gazette.com/pg/05243/563080.stm>.

Chapter 3. Flight From Danger
1. "Hurricane Katrina Advisory Number 19." National Oceanic and Atmospheric Administration, 27 Aug. 2005. NHC.NOAA.GOV, 18 Oct. 2006 <http://www.nhc.noaa.gov/archive/2005/pub/al122005.public.019.shtml?>.

2. "Statement on Federal Emergency Assistance for Louisiana." The White House Office of the Press Secretary. 27 Aug. 2005. 11 Nov. 2006 <http://www.whitehouse.gov/news/releases/2005/08/20050827-1.html>.

3. Gordon Russell. "Mayor Orders First-Ever Mandatory Evacuation of New Orleans." *New Orleans Times-Picayune*. 28 Aug. 2005. NOLA.com (weblog). 19 Oct. 2006 <http://www.nola.com/newslogs/breakingtp/index.ssf?/mtlogs/nola_Times-Picayune/archives/2005_08.html#074564>.

4. Ibid.

5. "Hurricane Katrina Advisory – Devastating Damage Expected." National Oceanic and Atmospheric Administration. 28 Aug. 2005. NHC.NOAA.GOV, 19 Oct. 2006 <http://www.srh.noaa.gov/data/warn_archive/LIX/NPW/0828_155101.txt>.

6. "Poor, Homeless, Frail Flock to Safety of Superdome." *USA Today*. 28 Aug. 2005. USAToday.com. 22 Oct. 2006 <http://www.usatoday.com/weather/stormcenter/2005-08-28-katrina-homeless_x.htm>.

7. Ibid.

8. Ibid.

9. Mary Foster. "Hurricane has Gulf Coast on the run; Massive evacuation under way as storm gains strength." Associated Press, 28 Aug. 2005, Proquest 23 Oct. 2006 <http://proquest.umi.com/pqdweb?did=888868501&Fmt=3&clientld=44099&RQT=309&VName=PQD>.

Chapter 5. Disaster
1. "Katrina Timeline" Think Progress. *ThinkProgress.org*. 2 Oct. 2006 <http://thinkprogress.org/katrina-timeline>.

2. "Latest Hurricane Katrina Developments - Escaping Through Roofs." *USAToday.com* (weblog). 29 Aug. 2005. 15 Oct. 2005 <http://www.usa today.com/weather/stormcenter/2005-08-29-katrina-blog_x.htm>.

3. "Breaking News - Hurricane Katrina Makes Landfall." *Cable News Network* (transcript). 29 Aug. 2005. CNN.com. 28 Oct. 2006 <http://transcripts.cnn.com/transcripts/0508/29/bn.02.html>.

4. David Ovalle. "Shelter-seekers find long lines, noisy conditions in Superdome." *Knight Ridder Tribune News Service*. 29 Aug. 2005. 1. Proquest, 5 Nov. 2006 <http://proquest.umi.com/pqdweb?did=888933061&Fmt=3&client Id=44099&RQT=309&VName=PQD>.

Chapter 6. Destruction
1. John McQuaid. "Katrina Trapped City in Double Disasters." *New Orleans Times-Picayune*. 7 Sept. 2005. 1. NOLA.com. 18 Nov. 2006 <http://www.nola.com/newslogs/breakingtp/index.ssf?/mtlogs/nola_Times-Picayune/archives/2005_09_07.html>.

2. "Latest Hurricane Katrina Developments - Word of Casualties." *USAToday.com* (weblog). 29 Aug. 2005. 15 Oct. 2005 <http://www.usa today.com/weather/stormcenter/2005-08-29-katrina-blog_x.htm>.

3. Doug MacCash and James O.Byrne. "Catastrophic Storm Surge Swamps 9th Ward, St. Bernard, Lakeview Levee Breach Threatens to Inundate City." *New Orleans Times-Picayune*. 31 Aug. 2005. 1. NOLA.com. 22 Nov. 2006 <http://www.nola.com/hurricane/t-p/katrina.ssf?/hurricane/katrina/stories/083005catastrophic.html>.

4. Jonathan Betz. "Haunting Screams from Attics and Rooftops." *WWLTV.com*. 28 Aug. 2006. WWLTV.com. 1 Dec. 2006 <http://www.wwltv.com/katrina/wwltv/reporters/stories//wwl082406tpbetz.2f05b0a8.html>.

Chapter 7. New Orleans Crumbles
1. Lester R. Daily. "Former FEMA Administrator Analyzes Post-Katrina Failures." *Tampa Bay Weekly*. 7 Dec. 2006. TBNWeekly.com. 15 Dec. 2006 <http://www.tbnweekly.com/content_articles/120706_pco-05.txt>.

2. "Katrina Timeline." *Think Progress*. ThinkProgress.org. 2 Oct. 2006 <http://thinkprogress.org/katrina-timeline>.

3. Evan Thomas."How Bush Blew It." *MSNBC*. 19 Sept. 2006. 2. MSNBC.com. 1 Dec. 2006 <http://www.msnbc.msn.com/id/9287434/site/newsweek/page/2>.

SOURCE NOTES CONTINUED

4. Transcript. *NBC Meet the Press*. 4 Sept. 2005. MSNBC.com. 3 Dec. 2006 <http://www.msnbc.msn.com/id/9179790/>.

5. Martin Smith. "The Storm." *Frontline*. 24 Nov. 2005. PBS.org. 28 Nov. 2006 <http://www.pbs.org/wgbh/pages/frontline///storm/etc/script.html>.

6. Will Haygood and Ann Scott Tyson. "'It was as if we were all pronounced dead'." *Washington Post*. 15 Sept. 2005. A1. Washingtonpost.com. 3 Dec. 2006 <http://www.washingtonpost.com/wpdyn/content/article/2005/09/14/AR200 5091402655.html>.

Chapter 8. A City in Turmoil
1. Joseph Treaster and Deborah Sontag. "Local Officials Criticize Federal Government over Response." *New York Times*. 2 Sept. 2005. NYTimes.com. 3 Dec. 2006 <http://www.nytimes.com/2005/09/02/national/nationalspecial/ 02storm.html?ex=1283313600&en=91dbb8fd6813e10a&ei=5089>.

2. "Order out of Chaos." *CBS News*. 11 Sept. 2005. 2. CBSnews.com. 30 Nov. 2006 <http://www.cbsnews.com/stories/2005/09/10/60minutes/ main832576_page2.shtml>.

3. Felicity Barringer and Maria Newman. "Troops Bring Food, Water, and Promise of Order to New Orleans." *New York Times*. 2 Sept. 2005. NYTimes.com. 3 Dec. 2006 <http://www.nytimes.com/2005/09/02/ national/nationalspecial/02cnd-storm.html?ex=1283313600&en= a144858313da66be&ei=5088&partner=rssnyt&emc=rss>.

4. Adam Nossiter. "New Orleans Mayor Issues 'Desperate SOS'." *Associated Press*. 1 Sept. 2006, Brietbart.com. 28 Nov. 2006 <http://www.breitbart.com/news/2005/09/01/D8CBN9OG2.html>.

5. Joseph Treaster and Deborah Sontag. "Local Officials Criticize Federal Government over Response." *New York Times*. 2 Sept. 2005. NYTimes.com. 3 Dec. 2006 <http://www.nytimes.com/2005/09/02/national/nationalspecial/ 02storm.html?ex=1283313600&en=91dbb8fd6813e10a&ei=5089>.

6. Transcript. NBC Meet the Press. 4 Sept. 2005. *MSNBC.com*. 3 Dec. 2006 <http://www.msnbc.msn.com/id/9179790/>.

7. "Thousands Dead." *New Orleans Times-Picayune* (weblog). 1 Sept. 2006. NOLA.com. 4 Dec. 2006 <http://www.nola.com/newslogs/breakingtp/index.ssf?/mtlogs/nola_Times-Picayune/archives/2005_08.html>.

8. Josh White and Peter Whoriskey. "Planning, Response are Faulted." *Washington Post*. 2 Sept. 2006. A1. Washingtonpost.com. 25 Nov. 2006 <http://www.washingtonpost.com/wpdyn/content/article/2005/09/01/AR20 05090102428_pf.html>.

9. "Mayor to Fed: Get off your asses." *CNN*. 2 Sept. 2005. CNN.com. 24 Nov. 2006 <http://www.cnn.com/2005/US/09/02/nagin.transcript/>.

10. "People on the Ground Hesitated." *CNN*. 13 Sept. 2005. CNN.com. 5 Dec. 2006 <http://www.cnn.com/2005/US/09/13/katrina.response/index.html>.

Chapter 9. Loss and Recovery
1. "American Morning." *CNN* (transcript). 29 Sept. 2005. CNN.com. 5 Dec. 2006 <http://transcripts.cnn.com/transcripts/0509/29/ltm.03.html>.

2. "President, Lt. General Honore Hurricane Katrina Relief in Louisiana." *The White House Office of the Press Secretary*. 11 Sept. 2005. Whitehouse.gov. 8 Dec. 2006 <http://www.whitehouse.gov/news/releases/2005/09/20050912.html>.

3. Tom Platchett. "Katrina Updates as they Come in." *WWLTV.com* (weblog). 6 Sept. 2006. WWLTV.com. 6 Dec. 2006 <http://www.wwltv.com/local/stories/WWLBLOG.ac3fcea.html>.

4. "What's in the New Orleans Water?" *ABC News*. 6 Sept. 2005. abc.go.com. 7 Dec. 2006 <http://abcnews.go.com/Health/story?id=1101220>.

Chapter 10. The Road Ahead
1. Kelly Knauer, ed. *Hurricane Katrina: The Storm that Changed America*. New York: Time Books, 2005. 99.

2. Scott Parks. "The Displaced: Go Back Home or Start From Scratch?" *Dallas Morning News*. 4 Sept. 2005. DallasNews.com. 10 Dec. 2006 <http://www.dallasnews.com/sharedcontent/dws/news/katrina/stories/090405 dnmetdisplaced.422cfa1.html>.

3. Rosanne Scrible. "New Orleans Residents Weigh Risks of Returning." *Voice of America*. 18 April 2006. VOAnews.com. 13 Dec. 2006 <http://www.voa news.com/english/archive/2006-04/2006-04-18-voa69.cfm>.

4. Matt Apuzza. "Judge Orders FEMA to Make Payments." *Associated Press*. 13 Dec. 2006. Yahoonews.com. 20 Dec. 2006 <http://news.yahoo.com/ s/ap/20061213/ap_on_go_pr_wh/katrina_housing>.

5. Brad Heath. "For New Orleans after Katrina, too many Night Remain Silent." *USA Today*. 21 Dec. 2006. USAToday.com. 28 Dec. 2006 <http://www.usatoday.com/news/nation/2006-12-20-new-orleans- rebuilding_x.htm>.

6. Ibid.

7. Cathy Booth Thomas. "New Orleans Today: It's Worse Than You Think." *Time*. 20 Nov. 2005. Time.com. 12 Dec. 2006 <http://www.time.com/time/ magazine/article/0,9171,1132832,00.html>.

INDEX

ABOUT THE AUTHOR

Jeannine Ouellette is the author of two books. She has published hundreds of essays and articles in national and regional magazines, and her work has been reproduced in several anthologies, including *Women's Lives: Multicultural Perspectives*.

She is the recipient of first place awards in writing and editing from the Medill School of Journalism, and the winner of a 2006 Page One Award from the Society of Professional Journalists for her magazine cover story on the dwindling population of honeybees and the healing properties of propolis.

PHOTO CREDITS

AP Images, 23; Charlie Riedel/AP Images, cover, title page, 78, 86; Andy Newman/AP Images, 6; NOAA/AP Images, 13; NOOA/AP Images, 24, 96 (top), 97 (top); Dave Martin/AP Images, 33, 34, 67, 68, 97 (bottom); Bill Haber/AP Images, 38; Vincent Laforet/AP Images, 41, 42, 99 (top); Gary Nichols/AP Images, 49; Eric Gay/AP Images, 50, 73; David Phillip/AP Images, 57, 60; Mari Darr–Welch/AP Images, 59; Rogelio Solis/AP Images, 77, 96 (bottom); Pat Sullivan/AP Images, 80; Jessica Kourkounis/AP Images, 85, 98; Rob Carr/AP Images, 89; Chitose Suzuki/AP Images, 92, 99 (top); Ric Ftancis/AP Images, 95; Phil Martin Photography, 14; National Oceanic and Atmospheric Administration (NOAA), 9